WRITE YOUR BOOK IN 24 HOURS!

WRITE YOUR BOOK IN 24 HOURS!

HOW TO WRITE, PUBLISH, AND PROMOTE YOUR BOOK, QUICKLY

MICHAEL JAMES FITZGERALD

OVERDUE BOOKS

Copyright © by Michael James Fitzgerald.

All rights reserved.

Printed in the United States of America.

First edition, August 2013 (rev. 20200708)

No part of this publication may be reproduced, stored in any retrieval system, or transmitted, in any form, or by any means, whether electronic, mechanical, photocopying, sound recording, or otherwise, without the prior written consent of the author, except as allowed by law.

E-book:

ISBN-13: 978-1-887309-17-9

ISBN-10: 1-887309-17-2

Paperback:

ISBN-13: 978-1-887309-16-5

ISBN-10: 1-887309-16-0

Quantity discounts for corporations and other groups available upon request.

CONTENTS

Introduction	1
Prep: Transcription	15
Prep: Finding an Editor	19
Prep: Sharing Audio Files with Your Transcriptionist	23
Prep: Setting Up Your Amazon Kindle Direct Publishing Account	25
Prep: Paperback and Hardcover Books	29
Prep: Self-publishing vs. Traditional Publishing	33
Prep: Start Creating a Book Cover	35
Prep: Set Up Social Media Accounts	41
Step 1: Figure Out What Your Book Is about	45
Step 2: Talking Points	49
Step 3: Recording Plan	53
Step 4: Dictating Your Book	59
Step 5: Assembling and Formatting Your Book	65
Step 6: Editing Your Book	69
Step 7: Publish and Promote Your Book	75
Pitfall Pit-stop	83
A Final Word	87
Appendix	93
About the Author	97
Also by Michael James Fitzgerald	99

Mark S. Fitzgerald
1955–2012

INTRODUCTION

I know it may seem impossible for you to write your book in 24 hours or less, but it's not.

Nothing is impossible unless you think it is. Everything is possible if you think it is.

I wrote this book in less than 24 hours, and I'm going to prove that you can write a book in 24 hours too by showing you step-by-step how to get it done.

I am not talking about jamming all 24 hours into a single day, but spreading the 24 hours over several days, a week, a month, or a year. I haven't written a book in 24 contiguous hours—in one day on the calendar—but I believe it's possible.

If you choose to write a book in 24 hours, it's not going to be easy. But it will be pretty cool.

I'm going to suggest you do some unusual things in the pages that follow. One supremely important thing: You're going to overthrow your body's subtle and relentless plot to keep you away from discomfort. You're going to have to tell your body to do exactly what your mind wants it to do.

Get ready for a challenge. And a huge reward.

When you complete the challenge, you'll be very excited and satisfied with your results! It will be worth all the effort and sacrifice.

Believe in Yourself

The first step to writing a book is believing in yourself. Not everyone will agree with me on that point but hear me out.

Have you ever suffered from writer's block, that leaden feeling that you can't type another word on your keyboard, that dark blue feeling that you can't write well enough to share what you have to say with the world?

I have a theory that writer's block is caused by not believing in ourselves enough to give ourselves permission to share our message with others.

What can you do about it?

I'll tell you what I do. I give myself the benefit of the doubt. I'm not too hard on myself. I cut myself plenty of slack. I don't take myself too seriously. I laugh at myself and at the situations I find myself in. I look at myself in the mirror and say, "You're going to make it, Mike. Hold on because you're going to make it."

When I am writing, I tell myself over and over, "Hey, you good looking guy, you can do this. You really can. Hang in there. Wait for the next word to come. It will be here soon. And don't forget: You can write as well as anyone else."

I say things like that to myself and I really mean it. I believe in myself, fall down, and rebelieve in myself. It's my modus operandi.

And I also forgive myself regularly and freely.

Forgive Yourself

Another thing that really contributes to writer's block, in my opinion, is refusing to forgive yourself. We all make mistakes and most of us make very stupid, serious mistakes that we are glad did not make it to the nightly news.

My advice is to not hold it against yourself, because if you don't forgive yourself, it is pretty solid evidence that you don't like yourself, and if you don't like yourself, you will constantly find fault with yourself. And if you are constantly picking yourself apart, it is likely that you will be reluctant to express yourself. With that comes a serious case of writer's block.

Fortunately, writer's block is not a terminal disease. It is fully curable.

In addition to believing in yourself, forgive yourself. Be nice to yourself. Love yourself. You are learning how to be a human being.

Nobody, not your parents, not your boyfriend or girlfriend, not your high school volleyball coach, can explain to you in comprehensive and believable terms what it takes to be a human. You have to learn the hard way. You have to graduate from the school of hard knocks.

These learning experiences are not easy. Life, fully lived, is not for wimps.

But you are not a wimp. You are still learning, so forgive yourself. Not just for that one big boo-boo you committed in the summer of 1987. Forget about that. Forgive yourself for that and for everything else. Don't hold back your forgiveness.

Self-acceptance is a doorway to forgiving yourself for the mistake's you've made. You will never fit in until you fit in with yourself. No one should be more accepting of yourself and forgiving of yourself than you, even though you've made mistakes and will continue to make them.

Tip: Forgiveness does not absolve you the from the responsibility to fix what you've broken, insofar as possible. But for what you can't fix yourself you have to rely on a power higher than yourself to resolve. Reach up for help. It is there.

Why Do You Want to Write a Book?

Why do you want to write a book? No question is more important at the moment than this one. You need to know the real reason why you want to do this, because your true, underlying motivation will be the strongest indicator of your future success.

I am not here to judge you, but if you are only after fame or a fast buck, don't bother.

I am not saying that you should only write for altruistic reasons. No, I'm not saying that. What I am saying is that if you are motivated to help other people first, before you serve selfish whims, you will be much more inclined to win the confidence of your readers.

If you want to share your knowledge with others; if you want to help others avoid the mistakes and pitfalls of life that you have learned the hard way; or if you want to share your story with others, then I believe you are on the right path. I hope you go for it!

How I Got Started

I started out my career as a writer a long time ago. It was 1983. I had just graduated from a university with a degree in English. A short time after that I got my first job as a technical writer for a big technology company. I enjoyed the work a lot. I still enjoy technical work. Because I enjoy it, I have written ten technical books—two for John Wiley and Sons and eight for O'Reilly Media—and I am in the planning stages for other technical books now.

I love what I do. I would do it even if I did not get paid to do it.

You may know some technical writers or people who were technical writers once upon a time. Most of the time people get worn out on technical writing. They quit and give up and move on to other careers.

I took a different path. I stuck with it. I really liked it and, because I like what I do, I have written a lot of books, technical and otherwise.

When will I stop? I have no plans to stop. I will never retire from writing. I'll keep doing it until I can't do it anymore.

Writing in a Journal

Another thing I've done to prepare for a writer's life is to keep a personal journal. I started keeping a personal journal when I was 18 years old. I wrote my first entry on April 20, 1976, and I've kept doing it ever since—year after year after year. At this moment, I have written over 8,000 pages and am on my 49th volume. I am writing in my journal every day now. This practice is woven into the fiber of my day-to-day life.

The reason why I keep writing in my journal is because I love to do it. I'm not sure if anyone will ever read my journals. That's not so important to me. I'm not writing those journals to have them published.

What I'm doing in my journal is expressing myself and that's what you'll do when you write a book. It's one of the greatest satisfactions of life—writing and producing something in book form. It's an unequaled opportunity to express yourself and to come to better understand yourself and to feel understood—or at least a little more understood.

Expressing Yourself

I recently heard the phrase "Inspiration minus expression equals depression."

Isn't that true?

Many times we have feelings inside of us— thoughts, ideas, dreams—and instead of *expressing* them we *suppress* them. It doesn't help us at all and, for certain, it doesn't help other people.

One thing about true inspiration is that as it comes to you, you want to share it, and when you share it, it always helps someone else. That's how you know it's the real deal.

This is your opportunity to share who you really are. I congratulate you for reading this book and I look forward to teaching you step-by-step how to get this book thing done in record time.

The Day It All Started

A lot of people would like to write a book but they're not really sure how. Let me tell you about a couple of experiences that may help.

One day when I was 18 years old, I was standing over a copy machine making copies of something I had typed up. A thought entered my mind, "You will write books one day." Perhaps those weren't the exact words that came to my mind, if any words came at all. It was more of feeling, like a vision, a vivid impression that warmed my mind and heart.

I knew it was something that would be important to my future.

I continued to nurture and hold that dream close to my heart. Finally, after many years of work as a writer, I started to publish books back in 1995. Since that time I have written more than 20 books and I don't see an end in sight.

So why do *you* want to write a book? What has happened to you in that past that brought you to this moment? What moments of inspiration have come to you? What kind of a book do you want to write? It's up to you.

You are a unique person. Nobody else in this world can be you. Nobody else can interpret this world or see this world like you do.

To find out why you would like to write a book, explore your thoughts. Get a notebook or open up a file on your computer or smart device and start taking notes. Write down your reasons why you want to write a book. Write at least 10 reasons down. Push yourself. 10 reasons.

Note: Even though we'll talk about creating paperback books, our main focus will be creating an e-book. Our goal is speed. We can get an ebook—cover and all—done very quickly. Then you can add a hardcover or paperback after that. Just laying some groundwork here.

Why You Can Write a Book

So why *can* you write a book? Many times I've met people who say things like, "I'm not a writer. I couldn't how to write." But the truth is that you can write and let me give you an example of why.

Are you willing you follow a little instruction? I recommend that you do it with your two legs. (If you're physically unable to do it with your two legs then do it in your mind.) Get up and walk across the room and then walk back.

Did you actually do it? Did you notice how easy that was? Why was it easy?

One of the reasons why is because it's something you've done your whole life. When you started out, it wasn't so easy, like back when you were a wobbly toddler. Over time you got better and better and better at it so that now you can walk with balance and grace everywhere you go.

Why did that happen? Well, you've had a lot of practice.

The same thing will work with writing. A lot of deliberate practice really helps you make progress. And there's lots of things you can do to accelerate that practice.

Tip: Writing over 8,000 pages in my personal journal was good practice. I highly recommend you take up journal writing if you want to be a writer of consequence.

If You Can Talk, You Can Write

Another thing that you're probably pretty good at is talking. You probably have a vocabulary of thousands of words that you can use and put together every day. Did you know that on average you can speak between 90 and 125 words per minute, depending on the setting or situation? It is said that women can speak more quickly than men and so women can have gusts of up to 175 words per minute. (This is probably because women have 40 percent or more connections between the hemispheres of their brains. It's true. Look it up.)

What if you were to transform your spoken word into the written word? Would that help to speed up the process a bit? It would. That's a method we're going to use in this book.

Getting Unstuck

Do you feel stuck in your life, like you can't move forward? Like you're walking around with a 200-pound backpack on your shoulders? Writing can help you get unstuck.

What makes you feel stuck is the anxious little ball of undefined feeling that lurks around the corner of your mind. You feel it is there. You know it is there. But you're not quite sure what it is.

You have to find a way to unplug your anxious, unconscious mind.

Writing connects your conscious mind with your unconscious mind. It takes a little practice, a little getting used to, but a way for your unconscious mind to find expression is through writing. Once you figure this out, you'll never suffer from writer's block again.

Disorder and Indecision

Disorder is a form of indecision. If you look around your environment and if you've got a lot of disorder, you know, you've got papers lying all over the place and pictures that haven't been hung on the wall and bills in a stack someplace in no particular order, it can be any form of disorder. A messy house, a cluttered refrigerator, all this is talking back to you and telling you that you have not made a decision.

One of the most important steps to making progress in your life is making decisions and making decisions quickly. People sometimes make decisions quickly, sometimes they make them over a long period of time, but one thing that I found is that if you are constantly in the process of thinking things through and deciding what it is that you really want in life, then your decisions come much more quickly.

If you find that your queue in your brain is clogged and you have a tough time sorting things out and making decisions, your brain is in a state of disorder it doesn't know how to function, it doesn't know how to respond to your commands because it's not sure what you really want.

I found it's very important to figure out what you *really* want and then make a very firm decision about getting that.

This applies to writing a book. Some people take a really long time to write a book. I have done that myself. One book took me 23 years to write and I have written other books in a very short period of time—like this book because of the methods that I'm using to write it. The difference between writing a book in 23 years and writing one in 24 hours is the quality of the decisions I've made.

I want you to succeed in writing this book. You're going to have make a lot of decisions and you're going to have to make them fast if you want the job done quickly. So I'll be guiding you and helping you to figure out what it is that you really want and to put some order in your life.

That's why you'll find a number of very specific steps in this book that you can take to accomplish this task. I've put them in order and I've laid them out in a way that you don't have to think hard about them. You can just start doing them and if you will just trust me and act decisively, you'll find that you will be able to accomplish the goal of this book. If you are mired in indecision and doubt (doubt is the fuel of indecision and disorder is the manifestation of it) then you won't be able to accomplish this. Doubt is a choice and it reveals your deepest desires.

My advice to you is to take each step at a time, get focused on one step at a time and just go after it. I'll show you easy ways to get things done. So good luck to you and I promise you that if you will follow these steps in the order that I give them and you'll follow them with energy and cast your doubts aside, you will accomplish this task.

Get Ready

I encourage you to prepare yourself mentally, emotionally, and spiritually for this major, upcoming life event: Writing a book. There are several things you can do to be prepared.

Number one, get ready to discipline yourself. If you really want to accomplish this in 24 hours, and I can prove to you that you can, you have to follow the instructions I give you precisely, with belief in self, and with energy.

Yes, you can and will adapt these instructions to your own way of doing things in the future, but for now, stick with me.

I'm sort of a drill sergeant for writers. But I'm your writing buddy, too. I'm not going to lead you astray.

If you read something that I suggest you do and you say to yourself, "Ah, I don't need that step," or, "Hmm, I'm not going to do that now," then you're not going to succeed. Nothing helps you more than when you commit yourself and follow through with your commitment and your conviction.

One way we follow through with our commitments is by getting our recalcitrant and otherwise lazy bodies to do what we tell them to do.

Many of the problems in the world today are a result of a sedentary, lazy, sullen lifestyle. People spend too much time staring at screens. They don't use their bodies; they don't use their minds like they could. So prepare yourself mentally to take on the challenges that you're about to face and discipline yourself to accomplish them.

Think big and stop playing small. Realize that there is much that you can do and say and think that will expand your world and expand the world of others. It doesn't matter where you are in life, what you've done, or what you haven't done: You have the divine ability to succeed. You have the ability to do this. You really do. And if you follow the pattern I'll show you, it's a mathematical impossibility to fail. If you do one step, two step, three step and you continue on to the end, you will succeed.

I repeat: It's a mathematical impossibility to fail—if you refuse to give up.

Consistent Persistence

You know the proverb about moving mountains with faith? What if someone asked you to move a mountain and you didn't feel spiritually, mentally, or physically able to do that? Then that person handed you a shovel and showed you the base of the mountain and said, "Start digging."

Now some mountains are absolutely huge, thousands of feet high, and thousands of feet in diameter at the base. But if you could live hundreds, maybe thousands of years ,and if you just continue to turn over that shovel and get a new shovel when you needed to, and shovel and shovel and shovel, you will eventually move that mountain. The key is consistent persistence, in not giving up.

Prepare yourself mentally and decide that you're not going to give up, you're not going to throw in the towel, that you will finish what you have begun.

A Few Cautions

To be completely honest and fair, it would be very difficult for you to write a book that you have never thought of writing. So I am assuming that you already have an idea that you may have nurtured and developed. It may feel somewhat incomplete in your mind, it may not be well-formed, but it is there.

Also, it would be difficult to write a work of fiction in 24 hours. You could do it, but novels benefit from planning, outlining, and rumination. Novels require time to develop. Novels need a gestation period. You could try it, but no guarantees from me, my friend.

It will also not work well for a book requiring research that you have not yet done. If in the writing process you have to do a lot of research, it ain't going to fly. Research can be very time consuming and distracting.

It also won't work well for history which requires a lot of footnotes and citations (though it will work fairly well for writing a personal history or memoir).

This method will work best if you are writing nonfiction, some kind of an instructional book, or the straight retelling of facts from your heart and memory.

Now let's talk about the secret weapon of really fast "writing." We'll start with transcription in the next chapter. (By the way, all the steps in the following chapters are also briefly restated in the appendix.)

PREP: TRANSCRIPTION

I'd like to tell you about how to hire a transcriptionist or enroll in a transcription service if you are dictating your book.

What I've done is gone out to and Upwork.com and found people to do the transcription for me. There are different job marketplace websites than Upwork, such as Guru.com, Elance.com, and Freelancer.com. You can find people that you can employ on an hourly or fixed-price basis. Assuming that you are writing your book in English, you can find great people who speak excellent English in all parts of the world and who can do excellent transcription work at a reasonable cost.

Tip: To really speed things up, you might hire more than one transcriptionist at a time.

You just go to one of these sites and register and do a little shopping. Search on the term *transcription* to look for somebody who can do transcription work. Look for ratings and a rate that you feel is fair and equitable and hire them. The latest transcriptionist that I hired, I hired him before I started actually dictating this book. I got it all set up so that as soon as I started dictating it I could send him the audio files and he could go to work.

Another option is to go with a web-based transcription service such as:

- Rev.com
- TranscribeMe.com
- GMRTranscription.com
- Scribie.com
- iDictate.com

They charge a per-minute or per-word fee. Shop their prices and decide for yourself. As of this writing, Rev.com, TranscribeMe.com, and iDictate.com also offer apps for your phone or other device so you can connect, dictate, upload, and pay all from your phone. Very convenient.

Tip: If you are traveling a lot and in a car and you have a smartphone, you can just get on the phone and start dictating using a voice recording app, then email or upload your audio files to the transcriptionist or the service. Or use one of the apps mentioned in the previous paragraph.

You can dictate is using the dictate option on Apple or Android products. I've used this service and it's surprisingly accurate—most of the time. I find though, that I have to dictate in a rather plodding or well-thought out and sometimes choppy way in order for this kind of dictation to work. It's not my favorite way to do dictation/transcription. It wouldn't be my first choice for dictation. To jot down some quick notes while I'm working, yes. But to a lengthy dictation, no.

It's the dictation step that will really save you most of the time because what happens is you get your files back and they're nicely formatted and you can just begin editing them and changing them and shape them into what you want. I have found that actually what I do dictate is very close to what I want but I can add to it and develop it once I get it back in written form. It's just a lot easier to edit text that I've dictated than to start from scratch if I'm writing a book quickly.

Tip: If you are on a Mac, you can try the dictation feature (see **System Preferences > Dictation & Speech**) to dictate your book. It is fairly accurate, but you have to dictate in chunks. You'll also need an Internet connection to do it.

Tip: Microsoft Word now has a **Dictate** option for a variety of languages. Try that out if you have a recent version of Word. It may work for your style, it may not. Direct dictation-to-transcription requires trial-and-error and patience.

PREP: FINDING AN EDITOR

The next thing you'll need to take care of is to find an editor. This is another preparation step.

A copyeditor usually is someone who will edit copy—text such as a manuscript for your book—and be able to identify the usage, grammar, and style errors. A copyeditor is not a developmental editor or a substantive editor as you would have in long-cycle editing.

Developing the text, making any substantive changes, looking at the larger structure, making a deep dive into your manuscript: that, among other things, is the work of a substantive editor.

Traditionally, a proofreader is a little different. A proofreader will generally read a text and then highlight areas where changes need to be made but generally does not make those changes. In the industry of editing, the proofreader often just marks those changes and then an editor will actually make them in the text. That would be you.

You may not be connected with someone who is a willing and capable proofreader, copyeditor. A solution to that is the same as getting a transcriptionist. What I would suggest is that you go to the same site (Upwork.com, Freelancer.com, etc.) that you chose to hire a transcriptionist.

You're going to have to work to develop a relationship with the person you hire. It's really great when you can develop a good relationship with a copyeditor or proofreader because then you can get a symbiosis. You understand each other's personalities and what to expect from each other. This is a relationship that will help you professionally for years if you do it right.

Use your best instincts to find someone who appears to have experience, who appears to have a good rating, be responsive, who's got good comments and good reviews on their work on the site. Take your best shot.

Like a transcriptionist, you want to get your editor in place *before* you start work so you can send them chunks of work (otherwise known as chapters) along the way. Let them know up front that this is how you want to work.

Tip: Hiring a good editor will be worth every penny you spend—every penny. They will save your neck from the chopping block.

When I help people publish books I really encourage them to make sure that they have the safety net of a copyeditor or a proofreader helping them as they create their text.

Tip: If you are an experienced writer or editor, one approach you can take if you are in a huge hurry or low on money is to carefully read your manuscript out loud to yourself. Reading aloud turns on different areas in your brain and helps you to "see" your errors more readily. Hiring an editor is safer and better, but use this method if you are in a tight spot.

Tip: One other method is to swear in a posse. Ask some literate and willing friends or family members in your circle who are excited about your project to do a search-and-destroy mission on typos in your book. Pay them a $1.00 bounty for every typo they find. This method could work well if you have teenage children who want to make an extra buck, want to be clever, and would love to have a little laugh at their parent's expense.

PREP: SHARING AUDIO FILES WITH YOUR TRANSCRIPTIONIST

Here is another prep step. If you are using a transcription service like Rev.com, you don't have to worry about this step.

At this point, if you are going to use a transcriptionist—a living, breathing person, your new BFF, who might not live on the same continent as you—you will need to get ready to send your files out to him or her.

Your audio files can grow to be quite large, and they are less practical to email, so use something like Google Drive (you have Google Drive if you have a Google account) to get the files to the person doing the transcription. You could use Dropbox.com, Box.com, or Apple iCloud or another file storage or cloud site that suits you.

If you already have a Google account (you have a Google account if you already have a Gmail account), it's your lucky day. You already have a Google Drive account. Look for the Google Drive icon and click it. Ta da. See. You're in business.

You share a folder with the person doing transcription and then copy your files to that folder. For example, in a Dropbox folder, right click on a folder you want to share and click **Share this Folder**.

Tip: Decide on a file naming scheme with your transcriptionist to help keep track of what goes where, for example, **01_chap.mp4, 02_chap.mp4**, etc.

Tip: It's good to check with your transcriptionist to make sure you know which type of online storage account will work best for them.

Tip: Keep copies of your audio files on your hard drive and thumb drive or an external drive. Make sure that you always make extra copies of the stuff that you dictate. Back up and protect your work. You'll be glad you did.

Tip: If you hire through Upwork.com, for example, you may be able to share the files through Upwork's built-in messaging system where you can upload files directly with messages.

PREP: SETTING UP YOUR AMAZON KINDLE DIRECT PUBLISHING ACCOUNT

Next I want to talk about another important preparation step: setting up your book on Kindle Direct Publishing (KDP), Amazon's publishing platform (kdp.amazon.com). Amazon Kindle revolutionized the world of publishing in late 2007 by making it really easy to publish and obtain ebooks—and now you can publish paperback books right along with your ebooks. More on that in the next chapter.

Kindle devices were first sold in 2007 as a way to deliver Kindle content. If you don't have a Kindle device, you can read books on the Kindle Cloud Reader (go to read.amazon.com) that works right in your browser, or a Kindle app for your desktop or laptop computer, phone, or tablet, making it possible for you to view Kindle content on a variety of devices.

There are a variety of ways to read and publish ebooks, but Kindle stands out as one of the most popular and easiest ways to publish and consume ebooks.

It's actually making some millionaires out there. John Locke, author of the Donovan Creed series of novels, was the first million-dollar writer/publisher back in 2011. His books are still selling on Amazon.

I've been publishing on Kindle since 2009. I've sold thousands of books and made extra income doing it. It's a fun platform and it's really easy to use.

You probably already have an Amazon account. If you do, login at kdp.amazon.com using your Amazon account login credentials.

When you bring up the KDP site, you'll see a little video that you can play to give you a quick idea of how it all works.

Now some of the advantages of Kindle is that you can keep control of your book. When you find errors, mistakes, and things that got overlooked, you can just go right back to the source file which you keep on the computer then upload it back to Kindle, and in a short time it will be available with the corrections in it. It's not a big deal to recover from errors.

You can publish your book all over the world in a matter of minutes really and it's pretty amazing. But it takes a little bit of time to get set up and approved, so I'm suggesting you start the process early. You don't have to push the Publish button just yet.

One of the benefits of Kindle is that you can earn a 70 percent royalty on your books. That's quite an improvement over traditional 10 percent royalties.

I have had 10 books published by traditional publishers. The first book I ever published through a traditional publisher was one I did through John Wiley and Sons, back in 2001. They gave me a generous advance on royalties and a 10 percent royalty rate. I had a good experience with John Wiley, but, though not long ago, the world has changed since then. A lot.

I also worked with O'Reilly, the technical publisher. I've had great experience with them and they offer a somewhat more generous royalty now, in their new model, where the ebooks bring you a 25 percent royalty – which is generous I think. But if you publish on something like Kindle, you're going to get a 70 percent royalty.

I encourage you to offer your books on other platforms as well in the future—for example, Apple using iTunes Connect at www.apple.com/itunes/working-itunes/sell-content/connect or on Barnes and Noble's site using press.barnesandnoble.com, Kobo.com, and Smashwords.com. But for right now, for the sake of speed and expediency, I am limiting my instructions to Kindle because it will get your book on the most popular book marketplace on the planet.

Tip: Supported upload formats include the following. You can learn more about the particulars of these formats here: kdp.amazon.com/en_US/help/topic/G200634390.

- Microsoft Word (doc/docx) — a preferred format
- Kindle Create (kpf) — a preferred format
- HTML
- MOBI and ePub
- Rich Text Format (rtf)
- Plain Text (txt)
- Adobe PDF

PREP: PAPERBACK AND HARDCOVER BOOKS

Now for the last prep step: In the past, you could offer a paperback version of your book using CreateSpace.com and easily associate it with your Kindle book because Amazon owns CreateSpace. Now CreateSpace has essentially been retired and KDP lets you publish both ebook and print-on-demand paperback at the same time.

What does print-on-demand mean? It means you can print books *after* they are ordered, not before. This is very different than what traditional publishing has commonly done: Books were printed in large quantities to get their unit costs down. But often publishers have to take back books, after the book had its initial chance at sales, usually in the first nine to 12 months of its availability. When sales die off, they often have to *remainder* the leftover books, meaning that the remaining books that were not sold would be returned to the publisher.

It was just a way that business was (and is) done and it's a hard thing. They used to have book stores that would just sell remaindered books, but I haven't seen one of these in a while. And part of the business also was figuring out a way to destroy those remaining books and certify that those books have been destroyed so that publishers could write those off on their taxes.

But now with print-on-demand, the order comes in for the book and *then* the book is printed so there's a big reduction in risk and resources. In other words, you don't have to put the paper and covers together until there is a clear demand.

By the Way: There is a machine out there that can produce a whole book (cover and interior pages) on the spot. It's called the Espresso Book Machine. It can create a book with a cover in a matter of minutes. One machine does everything. You can find out more at ondemandbooks.com. A local university in my area has one.

Self-publishing vs. Traditional Publishing

I realize that there is some thought that a self-published writer cannot enjoy the same prestige as someone who's published by a third party such as a famous New York publisher. I really don't think that's true anymore.

I think once a upon a time it was, but the state of publishing is very different now and one of the reasons why it is so different is that recently there's an interesting phenomena happening where (1) electronic book sales are outstripping the sale of bound, physical books, and (2) some of these ebook authors are making millions of dollars selling their books independently, such as John Locke who I mentioned previously.

These writers are being discovered by traditional publishers *after* they publish their work independently. Some are being offered buckets of money by these publishers, but turning them down because they don't see any financial advantage to signing a contract with a big name publisher (but some do).

Why? They have already established themselves. They are selling, some of them, thousands of units per month and they have a stream of income—a big, fat stream—and they don't need additional publishing help from the brick-and-mortar publishers, thank you very much.

And one of the reasons why is that they're selling their books cheaply but selling them in large quantities. Plus they keep 70 percent of their receipts as royalties rather than they 10 or 12 percent that a traditional publisher often offers a writer.

I think premier writers with traditional publishing who sell millions of copies of books get benefits beyond a royalty of 10 or 12 percent, but others are not quite so fortunate.

Independent writers who have fought and struggled to find their way and navigate through professional publishing houses and have been rejected countless times are now finding a place where their voices can be heard. (I know one author personally who had been rejected 1,000 times before going the self-published route.)

Sometimes their manuscripts become real books and they've self-published them and haven't done very well. But some authors, an increasing number of authors, are enjoying great success by publishing their own books using:

- KDP.Amazon.com
- iTunes Connect (see www.apple.com/itunes/working-itunes/sell-content/connect)
- Press.BarnesandNoble.com
- Kobo.com
- Smashwords.com

Or they might sell plain old PDFs or epub files their own websites just using shopping cart technology, which is easier than ever now with site like Shopify.com, among others (ecommerce sites are out of scope for this book).

Tip: If you want to learn more about writing sales copy, I recommend Robert Bly's *The Copywriter's Handbook,* 3rd edition, and *Words that Sell,* revised and expanded edition, by Richard Bayan.

Book Templates

This is a good time to either create or download a book template.

If you'd like to download a Word book template, you can find different sizes that I've made at www.michaeljamesfitzgerald.com/resources.html. All for free.

To format your book for Kindle, I would use the guide on the Kindle Direct Publishing site called "Simplified Formatting Guide" (you'll find it at kdp.amazon.com/self-publishing/help?topicId=A17W8UM0MMSQX6).

You can also download the free Kindle ebook *Building Your Book for Kindle* (www.amazon.com/Building-Your-Book-Kindle-ebook/dp/B007URVZJ6/).

There also is one for Macintosh computers, *Building Your Book for Kindle for Mac* (www.amazon.com/Building-Your-Book-Kindle-book/dp/B00822K3Z0/).

PREP: SELF-PUBLISHING VS. TRADITIONAL PUBLISHING

This book leads you through the steps of self-publishing a book. Let's take a few minutes to compare self-publishing with traditional, New York, high-rise publishing.

I realize that there is some sentiment that a self-published writer cannot enjoy the same prestige as someone who's published by a third party such as a traditional publisher. Psst. I really don't think that's true anymore.

There are millionaire self-publishers out there now. The number would probably surprise us. (I don't know what that number is.) They've figured something out. You got to give them a lot of credit for that.

I think once a upon a time it was, but the state of publishing is very different now and one of the reasons why it is so different is that recently there's an interesting phenomena happening where (1) electronic book sales are outstripping the sale of bound, physical books, and (2) some of these ebook authors are making millions of dollars selling their books independently.

These writers are sometimes being discovered by traditional publishers *after* they publish their work independently.

Some are being offered buckets of money by these publishers, but turning them down because they don't see any financial advantage to signing a contract with a big name publisher. This is not always the rule. These independent successes may work out new deals with traditional publishing. A mix of self and traditional publishing are common.

Why would a successful indie author decline lucrative offers by established publishers? Well, they have already established themselves. They are selling, some of them, thousands of units per month and they have a stream of income—a big, fat stream—and they don't need additional help from the brick-and-mortar publishers, thank you very much.

And one of the reasons why is that they're selling their books cheaply but selling them in large quantities. Plus they keep 70 percent of their receipts as royalties rather than they 10 or 12 percent that a traditional publisher often offers a new or less experience writer.

Some successful writers who publish through traditional publishing and sell millions of copies of books get benefits beyond a royalty of 10 or 12 percent, but others are not quite so fortunate.

Independent writers who have fought and struggled to find their way and navigate through professional publishing houses and have been rejected countless times are now finding a place where their voices can be heard. (I heard of one author personally who had been rejected 1,000 times before going the self-published route.) 1,000 times! That's determination. What a gift!

Sometimes authors—an increasing number of authors—are enjoying great success by publishing their own books using Kindle or iBooks or Nook or Kobo or Smashwords or even plain old PDFs, sold off their own websites just using a PayPal **Buy Now** button.

PREP: START CREATING A BOOK COVER

Next, begin creating a book cover or get someone to create it for you. Start early on this process.

A book cover can be extremely simple, but it should be eye catching and hold promise for the buyer. I'm going to talk first about a simple cover. To make a simple cover, go to Canva.com and sign up for a free account. Then select **Create a design**, then **Book Cover** and have some fun. Use fonts and different font sizes to create or discover a reasonably simple yet appealing look.

I get inspiration from looking at other book covers. For example, just today, I went to Amazon and looked at the top 100 bestselling books in Business and Money to find covers I liked.

You can hire someone to create your book cover as well. I'll show you how to do that in a moment.

I've made a number of book covers myself and I'm getting better at it. But I don't recommend this to everyone. I started out making really amateur looking covers and they don't help sell books. Trust me on that one. I've been publishing books since 1995 and have made plenty of embarrassing mistakes. But

I've picked up some skills over the last few decades and they are working for me now. But it took awhile.

There is an another way to create a cover if you publish on KDP: There you will find a cover creator feature that allow you to create decent—well, sort of okay—book covers (front covers for Kindle book and full covers for paperback books) at no cost. The instructions are simple and the results will be sufficient, but will not match the work of a professional designer and their tools.

Yet another option is Fiverr.com. Go to Fiverr, search for "book cover design" and start scrolling. You'll quickly find folks from all over the globe who can make you a good-looking book cover and that will work for any budget.

More options on cover design will follow. For now, you have to have something to put on the cover—that is, a title and subtitle.

Your Working Title

Here you have to come up with a list of working titles, one or two at least. The title doesn't have to be set in stone at this moment, but you'll need *something* to put on your cover. Then, try to create at least five potential covers on Canva or in the KDP cover creator, then push yourself to do a few more. Ruminate on your list of titles and come back to it over a break to take a fresh look at them. What pops for you> You want something that will stand out.

Consider the title of former-Navy SEAL operative Clint Emerson's book, *100 Deadly Skills*. Did that just get your attention, in either a positive or negative way? That's the idea. You want to grab potential readers by the lapels, at lest for 1-2 seconds. Make that your goal. Ask, Is my title a lapel grabber? If the answer is yes, you're on the right track.

Tip: When I am struggling with a working title, the name of a character, or something like that, I want to be open to and play with ideas. I will open a notebook or a computer file and begin jotting down titles, names, or what have you. I might write down 20 or more. Then I go back and highlight or star the ones I like the best, and pick the one that jumps off the page for me. This is not work for me. It's my kind fun.

ISBNs

When we start our own little publishing company, it was less expensive to get ISBNs—International Standard Book Numbers. They are more expensive now than when I got my batch. I'm still using the original list 10-digit ISBNs that I got way back in 1995 though I have to convert them to 13-digit ISBNs now. I keep care of that list in a special file because it's valuable.

It's great to have those numbers because, as I said, they were a lot less expensive to get back then than than they are now. But you don't need to have an ISBN to publish a book on Kindle. However, you will need an ISBN for a paperback on KDP.

Getting Bids on Cover Design Work

Let me tell you how I got a cover for a novel. There's several websites out there—for example, 99designs.com, CrowdSpring.com, DesignCrowd.com—where you can register for an account and put out a bid for a book cover or a logo or any kind of a design you like. And you can tell them you want to spend $100, $200, or $300 (or much more) on this design and put it up for a bid. Give it a good description and you'll find in a very short period of time dozens and dozens of proposed designs popping up, all vying for your attention and favor.

Many will go to the effort of creating mock-up design for your book cover and after giving it some time, you can select a book cover you want—whatever looks best to you—then pay for it. You'll find designers from all over the world, especially new and upcoming designers who are very hungry for work. But you'll find many of them are very talented and skilled. It's fun discovering those diamonds in the rough and I've discovered a few of them over the years.

Tip: You may know someone like this: I am personally acquainted with a graphic artist who is extremely talented. I've seen some of the book covers she's designed and I think they're world class. She is also very reasonably priced. For example, for a simple book cover like I'm doing myself for this book, she told me that she would just do it for $300. You may have someone in your circle like her who is the best option for you.

What's important if you are going to do this more than once is that you develop a network of people who can do work for you and with you. As you do more and more books, you'll find that you can do things in parallel, meaning that you'll be able to do several things at once when you've got a team, people who are helping you along the way.

You can do the cover of a well-planned book before you write the first word of the manuscript. Just saying.

So get out there and get that cover designed—either by yourself or by a crowd- sourced designer or a designer in your circle.

You can't *tell* a book by its cover but you can certainly *sell* a book by its cover. Ask friends and family in your circle for an honest opinion. You don't want a homespun cover. It doesn't have to be a Picasso; it just has to do its job: sell the book in 1 second.

Tip: If your pockets are well lined, you might try this. It would take more time than this project will allow, but you *could* create your own design bid system among designers you already know. Write up a few brief rules, offer a kill fee for an easy exit, and ask for bids. (A kill fee is a mutually agreed upon amount of money that you will pay. For example, let's say you personally know four designers. Tell them you are looking for a book cover and want to look at several comps before choosing a designer. Let each designer pull together a comp. Compare them and pick your favorite, and award your contract to the one you like best.

Tip: If you create your own cover, make sure you add 0.125" of bleed on each edge, plus allow for the width of the spine. To calculate the width of a spine, use a spine calculator. Look up "book spine calculator" in your favorite search engine.

PREP: SET UP SOCIAL MEDIA ACCOUNTS

You can set up accounts on the following sites in order to promote and market your book later on. This is optional. You don't have to do this step. You may want to wait until *after* your book is done to this, but each account takes about five or ten minutes to set up. (If you are savvy, you can give your self less than five minutes per site.)

I won't go into detail on how to set up or use these sites. They are self-explanatory, and there are web sites and books galore dedicated to social media if you need help with them.

> **Tip:** The easiest way for you to sign up on some of these accounts may be via a smart phone through apps of the same name from an app store.

Setting up an accounts on Twitter, Facebook, Pinterest, and so forth is very simple. You just go to site and click the **Sign Up** button or something similarly named. Enter a few pieces of personal information and you're in.

Believe me, these sites are all about making it as easy as possible to sign up and start sharing.

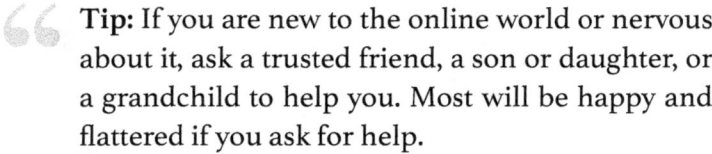
Tip: If you are new to the online world or nervous about it, ask a trusted friend, a son or daughter, or a grandchild to help you. Most will be happy and flattered if you ask for help.

Get on the Internet and use your favorite browser to go to the following sites (as many as you can) and get started:

- Facebook.com
- Twitter.com
- Pinterest.com
- SlideShare.net
- Instagram.com
- LinkedIn.com
- YouTube.com
- WordPress.com
- Blogger.com
- Tumblr.com

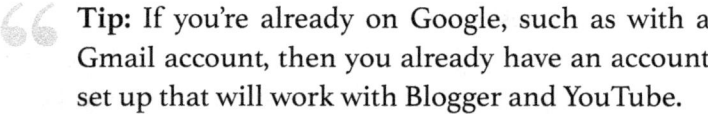
Tip: If you're already on Google, such as with a Gmail account, then you already have an account set up that will work with Blogger and YouTube.

These are among the most popular and effective social sites, but there are others. Use what works for you.

Tip: Picking a good username is important if you want to establish yourself independently as an author. You may try to set up a username and then find out that it is already taken. You can use your name and then add some unique word to it like *author* or something like that. Have fun but don't pick a schmaltzy username that goes thud and gives people the idea you're in middle school

—but if you are in middle school, disregard this schmaltzy advice. Just be your teenage self.

Start telling the world about your book. Ask your friends to like your page and start spreading the word. Let people know about your book, when it will be published, where they can find it, and what special offers you are making.

But be warned, you don't want to be one of those people whose only purpose on social media is to yell, "Buy my book! Buy my book!" You want your book to be part of your natural online conversations, part of who you are. Don't be an online, door-to-door sales rep. Be out there to help people. Offer free stuff, promotions, etc. that make it easy from people to get interested. Nothing forced or rah-rah.

> **Tip:** Go to the bottom of your home Facebook page and you'll notice a **Create a Page** link. That **Create a Page** link will take you to a place where you can enter all kinds of information about your book business or whatever else you're doing. What you can do is put a picture of your book cover or a mock up of the cover or something like that on your page. Get that uploaded and get going.

Don't be too salesy. Share your writing work with enthusiasm but don't act like all you care about is selling your book. That can be a big turn off and can counter your message. On the contrary, let people know you are a benevolent force in the universe, that you are solid and secure, that you are not going anywhere, and that you have something of value to share and that you are willing to make an exchange for what you have.

If you are too salesy, you will lose friends and fail to influence people and Dale Carnegie will not be happy with you.

Let people know that you care more about them than you care about your own interests. If you make that clear, you will be seen as trustworthy and will attract much more business in the long run.

Share with the intent to bless and uphold others, not to just uphold or glorify yourself, and it will surprise you how far it will take you. You have to give first before you receive. That's takes self-confidence, faith, and patience, but it works. Nothing else works to produce long-term, positive results.

Confession. I have been on social media since 2008 and have learned what works for me and what doesn't. I have a very limited presence there now. I mean *very*. However, some writers love to be on social media and use it very effectively. I am not one of those writers, but you may be. In any case, I wish you success, however you choose to pursue it.

STEP 1: FIGURE OUT WHAT YOUR BOOK IS ABOUT

Now you're going to do three things:

1. Choose a topic for your book. (I hope you've already been thinking about that. I'd bet you have.)
2. Make a plan on how and when you're going to write —create—your book.
3. Develop an outline for your book from a list of random talking points.

I'll start with choosing a topic.

Choosing a Topic for a Non-fiction Book

When I say you can write a book in 24 hours, that doesn't mean that you wake up fully clothed at 12:01 a.m. and begin writing and push the Publish button at 11:59 that night. I'm also not suggesting that you just pick a new topic out of the blue that you don't know anything about. What you need to do is pick a topic that you already know something about, one that you already feel comfortable with, one that you can yak and yank about.

Hmm. Did I just hear you say, "I don't know anything about anything." It's simply not true. You are an expert at something, even though you may not realize it.

One of the things I've already suggested is that you're probably an expert at walking. You don't recognize it because you do it every day.

So pick a topic that's familiar. I picked a topic for this book, that is, obviously, how to write and publish a book in 24 hours. This is something I know about. This is something that I'm comfortable with. This is something that I can talk about for hours on end with ridiculous enthusiasm.

What do you know about? What are you excited about? What can you comfortably talk about? Those are things you can write about. If you can talk about it, you can write about it.

A great way to determine a good subject for your book is by asking a question and answering that question. For example, this book that you're reading right now is answering the question, "How in the world can I quickly write and publish a book to meet a certain deadline?"

And so this book spans a number of pages to answer that question in some detail. What people really want is information that they value but don't have. Let me repeat that: What people really want is information that they value but don't have.

You have high quality information that other people don't have. No matter what point you're at in life, you have had experiences that have given you information that is not broadly understood by others, so others want what you have.

Let me give you some examples. In your life you may be experienced with bow and arrow; you might be experienced with selling cars; you might be experienced with raising disabled children; you might be experienced with overcoming addictions; you might be experienced with talking someone out of committing suicide. Who knows what you've experienced? Whatever it is, others in the world want and need the information you have. Trust me.

Your experiences and your personality are unique. You can turn your experience and your personality into a book.

You often hear people say, "I've got a book in me." I think that's true of every single person on this planet. Probably multiple books, really. Even if they don't have the desire or willpower to write, they still have a book (or more) inside of them.

If you sit and listen to a person's story—if they're willing to tell it—you'll be fascinated. It doesn't matter if you're a homeless person on the street or if you feel like you've lived an ordinary life, you will find that you have had unique and fascinating learning experiences that are worth retelling and worth sharing with other people who can learn and grow from your story.

Great subjects come from great questions.

Think about questions that you can or would like to answer.

- How did you recover from lost love?
- How did you overcome a cocaine habit?
- How did you ace that calculus exam?
- How did you face colon cancer?
- How do you rappel down a shear rock face?
- How do you write a book?

Target Your Audience

Who is your target audience? Who do think will be reading your book?

Look at your subject matter. To whom will it appeal?

Teenage girls ages 12–16 who like horses and who live in the United States? Middle-aged men with bad golf swings?

I suggest having a picture in your mind of you will actually read your book. The more specific you can be, the more likely you will appeal to that audience.

In 3 to 5 sentences, create a written avatar of an idealized reader, with as many details as you can imagine. Make them as real as you can in your mind then figure out how to serve that person with your words. Your beautiful, unique, powerful words. And while you're at it, love that person.

Now Hatch a Plan

You now have to make a plan. If you want to move forward, you've got to plan to do the job and plan how to do it.

What I suggest is that you have a plan essentially for each hour of the 24 hours and have three or more actions to take in each one of those hours. What that does is (1) breaks the work down to simple steps; and (2) it provides an organized flow.

You want to free your mind from the natural tendency to pause and think and to get worked up over details by organizing and sorting things beforehand. You want to know exactly what you're going to do when your feet are in the blocks and you hear the gun go off.

You've got to take into account what time you have to devote to this. Even though you may have very little time, you can still *make* time to talk into a microphone while you're in the car, crocheting an afghan, taking a walk, or putting on makeup—this is a technique I'm going to share with you a couple chapters from now. Before we get there, we'll discuss talking points—baby steps toward an outline.

STEP 2: TALKING POINTS

The next step is to develop an outline. It is an outline for all intents and purposes, but I think it starts out as a list of *talking points*.

An easy way to outline is to open a file on your computer in a favorite text editor. It doesn't matter what it is. It could be Word, Notepad, TextMate, OneNote, Bear, whatever. It could be any text editor; it doesn't really matter.

Then start typing simple lines of text describing the ideas you have and the points you want to cover in your book. Be as disorganized and crazy as you can be. Capture the ideas as rapidly as they come to your mind. Type like a crazy person.

The point is that in your first attempt, you don't want it to be organized at all. Just start spilling out the ideas. You want chaos. Just open up a vein and bleed out what's in your mind and put it down in electronic form so you can start on your path of sharing it with others.

It can be any sort of talking point. It doesn't have to be well-thought out. Not yet.

Nothing has to sound profound, nor does it have to be

arcane. Just let it be whatever it is and let it come out, then capture it and get it down.

You'll find that these ideas will take on a life of their own and start presenting themselves to you at odd moments. They'll pop into your head and you won't know where they came from. You need to be open and ready to receive them and write them down.

One key point in writing is accepting the words as they come, with no prejudice. Just accept.

Order out of Chaos

Let's say that you've listed 25 points. Look at them carefully for a few minutes and set them aside for an evening. Then take a look at them the next day. What will happen is as you submit these points to your brain, your subconscious mind will take over and it will start organizing and figuring out how the items on your list fit together.

When you get up the next morning, before launching off into your regular daily schedule, take a moment to look at the list you wrote, your talking points. Start to place them in order. Decide which is the first point you want to cover, which is the second, which is the third, and so on.

To me, it's kind of like staring at a chess board. I don't know if you've played chess or not, but sometimes you can stare at a chess board for a long time. You keep staring, staring, staring, and you're not sure what to do, what your next move will be. But it will come to you if you are patient and observant.

If you give it enough time, you will get little moments, epiphanies so to speak, and you will be able to figure out and organize your statements into a coherent whole.

Enjoy yourself, have fun writing your book, play with your ideas, play with your talking points and then shuffle them around.

Not all of them will be winners. Pick some of the ones that your most passionate about and start talking about them. Start talking about them with energy, start talking about them with love, and you'll be amazed what your heart and mind will produce.

Finalize Your Talking Points

Your talking points really are the outline of the book, as I wrote earlier.

We talked about this earlier—getting that started and letting your mind be free and just putting down everything you could think of without imposing a particular order. Let me ask you to do something else about that: Finalize the order of the things you want to talk about.

Look at your list and, in whatever file format you've got it in (I assume you probably use something like Microsoft Word or some other tool), organize those things as best you can in a logical order, in the way you'd best like to present them.

If you are writing a book of instructions, it could be the logical order of steps to accomplish a task. If you write a personal memoir, use a chronology of steps to guide the final order of your talking points.

Optional: Use Colored Sticky Notes

One way you can organize your talking points is by using colored sticky notes, like the 3-inch square size. I learned this skill from Geoff Affleck (GeoffAffleck.com). Dedicate a color to a certain area or topic and then use a wall or whiteboard to organize your thoughts. For example, you could choose a color for a principle or a main point, another for a statistic, another for a citation, another for a quote, and so forth. This kind of organization may come natural to you. If it's natural, go for it.

Whatever makes sense to you should make your job easier and help you save time.

Optional: Make Slides

And once you're satisfied with you talking points, I have another suggestion: Take your talking points and move them into a slide presentation, such as in Microsoft PowerPoint, Apple's Keynote, or Google's Presentation, available through Google Drive. (If you have a Google account, you already have Google Drive.)

Make a full presentation for live presentations and one or more abbreviated presentations for promotion. You can use abbreviated versions as part of your online promotion or advertising for the book.

A place that you can share these slides—after your book is published—is a site called SlideShare.net. I've got several accounts on SlideShare and, at the moment, my slide presentations get thousands of views with no promotion at all.

I've put slide presentations up there and they have been found by others simply by organic search. And so you can create a slide presentation based on your talking points and then at the end of the slides or various places in the slides you can add links or information to where you can find the book.

This step is optional and depending on the amount of material you have to present, you will want to wait until after you are done writing and publishing your book to create slides.

Next, let's talk about getting your thoughts from the idea stage to the sentence and paragraph stage, as soon as possible.

STEP 3: RECORDING PLAN

The next thing to do is set goals for how you will record yourself talking your book. That's right—talking your book.

If you want to fly, this is your next move, so start flapping. Your wings if you have them, but mostly your mouth.

If you want to get this done, you're going to record yourself yakking over your talking points, in logical order, and that's how you're going to "write" your book. Remember, we're wanting to get this done in 24 hours.

You know better than anyone what your schedule is like and where you can fit the time in to record your book.

It is best to set a clear goal with a target date for publication. Then I suggest you write this goal down on a piece of paper, in big letters, and hang it up where you can see it every day, maybe in several places.

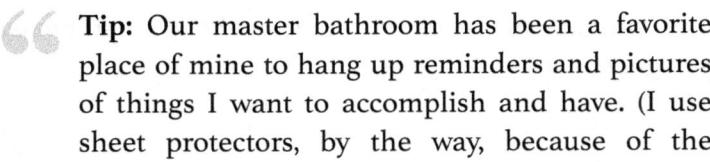

Tip: Our master bathroom has been a favorite place of mine to hang up reminders and pictures of things I want to accomplish and have. (I use sheet protectors, by the way, because of the moisture.) I created the first cover of this book early in the process, hung a print out of it in our master bath. I saw it often and was reminded of my goal. It helped me reach this goal—as you can see by reading this book.

Mental Tug of War

One of the big, fat lies we tell ourselves is we don't have time for the things we know we should do. We have a tug-of-war within ourselves. Half our brain talking in behalf of our body, the other half talking for our mind and spirit.

Your body is always saying, "I need a break. I need some rest. I want to relax. I gotta to hide from all the pressure. I want TV and caffeine and chocolate."

If you let it, your brain will serve the body and make you a slave of indulgence, but what you want is your brain and your body to become the servant of your mind and spirit. One of the ways you do that is by setting exciting, even scary, but worthwhile goals, and remind yourself of those goals often. Set them, write them down, and pursue them. With persistence and consistency, you'll be able to get your book written and published. Without persistence, slapping your own face, and self-insistence on something better, higher, and of more value, you can't accomplish much beyond survival.

And what often happens is, when you persist, you will find that you will accelerate. When your brain and body become obedient to your mind and spirit, that's when things start to really happen. And you also find ways to shave off time and to spend less energy.

Your spirit and mind are your brain and body's best friends. They might not know that yet. Let them know.

When to Record Your Book

You'll need a recording device. I'll talk about choosing a recording device a little later.

This is how I do it, if you'd like to know.

I sit down in front of my computer in the morning and at night—early in the morning before I go to work and after I come home from work, often late in the evening. Those are the times that work for me. Saturday is also a great time for me to do this kind of thing.

Usually, my goal is to record for five minutes at a sitting. Sometimes I go 10 minutes, sometimes a little longer, sometimes shorter, but five minutes is my regular goal.

I could go much longer but I choose to take on this effort in small bites and it works out well for me. It's amazing how much you can get done in a short period of time if you are persistent in following a schedule. These two qualities are what make a difference to me.

For example, you probably have a regular day job, like me (right now, I'm managing outsourced talent for a large, multinational corporation). If you've got to commute to your job—whether you're driving a car or walking—you could record your book during those times.

Keep Track of Your Time

As I recorded my book and spent time working on it, I noted the time that it's taking me to do it because that's part of the economy of the whole thing. How much time has it actually taken me to write and prepare this book? I ask myself that all the time. And I want to know the answer.

(By the way, I planned, dictated, wrote, edited, created, and published this book in 23 and a half hours.)

You'll find that in a short time you'll discover efficiencies that you did not consciously create. Your subconscious mind will be working through this and figuring out ways to get the thing done.

Your body will do what you tell it to do, eventually, all the while creating minimal pathways, reducing energy costs, and delivering more and more good ideas and clever techniques to your mind's doorstep. Listen and obey your higher mind. It's when you don't listen and don't obey that pure voice that you mess up in life.

Like I said, it's a tug of war, really, writing a book or doing anything that takes consistent effort. This is what happens when we are unconscious of this war: Our body will try to take over. You see this all around you all the time. People do not engage in healthy activities or are not engaged in moving forward with their lives because they have given in to the body and given up on their dreams. And they are miserable most of the time and hard to be around. Don't be that person.

That doesn't mean that we can't change. It doesn't mean that we can't change this minute, *today*. It doesn't mean that you and I can't change. But what it requires is for us to make clear, distinct, conscious efforts to *command* ourselves, to command our brains and our bodies, to be in submission to our higher selves and to what we want to accomplish in this life.

That's what it is going to take to get this job of writing a book done. There is, as Euclid (323–283 BC) said, no royal road or shortcut to geometry or to accomplishing any great, worthy task.

Recording Methods

Now let's choose a recording device or method. You've got to use something that's going to be easy for you to use. You're going to look for something that you can work with, an electronic device that you can record with that can record MP3 or MP4, MOV or WAV files.

You can easily go to a store like Target or Wal-Mart and find a selection of recording devices for as little as $30 – I've got one of those myself. Or you can go to Amazon and get something fancy and expensive.

But the important thing is not to get the highest quality recording device: The important thing is to just get started and to figure out what you're going to do.

> **Tip:** Jump over obstacles. Don't create them. You create obstacles when you take too much time making decisions about things like recording devices. It is best to act on a reasonable decision and then improve on your original decision *later* or *next time*. It is not best to hesitate and flounder.

If you're on the move, if you really don't have time to sit down in front of your computer and use it's recording capabilities. Get one of these hand-held devices or just use your smartphone and take it with you in the car. Imagine that: recording your entire book while driving to and from work—it can be done. I haven't done it that way for a whole book, but I've recorded a lot of stuff in the car. It could be done and it could be fun.

Anyway, choose a recording device and don't get too hung up on it but choose well. Choose something that will work and flow well with your workflow. To work well, you've got to be able to export the files quickly and easily.

I'll tell you what I do. I've got an Apple MacBook Pro laptop and I have the latest version of QuickTime player which is free and I use a headset or earbuds that plugs into the audio port that gives me headphones and microphone. I just put that headset on, plug it in, and then in QuickTime I go to **File** and I select **New Audio Recording**. That brings up a little box with a red circle. I click on that and start recording.

When I'm done recording, I export the files out of it using the **File Export** command and save them as MP4 files to a directory on my computer. Then I share them with my transcriptionist via Dropbox. It's as simple as that.

I'll tell you more about using dictation and transcription in the next chapter.

STEP 4: DICTATING YOUR BOOK

Let's talk for a few more minutes about the advantages of recording your book in audio format for transcription. This is where you'll get the most efficiency in writing your book. Let me explain.

Typing vs. Dictation

A good writer with years of experience can usually write on average approximately two pages of text in about an hour, that is, of new, original text. Sometimes a writer may write more, even a lot more, and sometimes less. But two pages of original text (between 500 and 600 words) is moving at a pretty good pace.

Let's say each one of those pages that he or she types is 286 words. That is the typical measure of typing guide pages (TGP) —a standard often used in translation where 286 words is an average word count for a page. So that means that, in an hour, an experienced writer can produce about 572 words. Let's be generous and round that up to 600 words.

So if you wanted to create a 100-page book and that's using

a typing-guide-pages word count of 286 words, that's 28,600 words. So if you use the typical writing method—for an experienced writer—that would take you approximately 48 hours to write.

Now let's take a little different approach, a little more speedy approach. If you speak into a microphone and you speak at a normal rate, you will speak between approximately 90 and 125 words a minute. If you're a fast talker, you can have gusts of up to 175 words per minute.

But let's just say conservatively that you're going to speak approximately 100 words per minute. Now take a low estimate on that. How does that translate into words? If you needed to get 28,600 words to hit 100 pages and you translated that into dictation time, let's see. 28,600 words divided by 100—it will take you 286 minutes to dictate that. That's 4.8 hours of dictation so about five hours of dictation.

In other words, it will take you about 10 percent of the time to dictate a book than to type it.

Dictation Options

What I'm saying is that you can dictate—speak your whole book—into some sort of a recording device. You might plug a microphone into your computer and use a tool like QuickTime where you can record a new audio recording. You can use a smartphone or handheld digital voice recorder and save it as a WAV, MP3, or MP4 file.

You might have a smart phone that has a dictation app that you could use. As mentioned earlier, you might use an online service or its app:

- Rev.com (has app)
- TranscribeMe.com (has app)
- GMRTranscription.com

- Scribie.com
- iDictate.com (has app)

There's a variety of things that you can do to record your voice.

So it's really up to you experiment with something that you're comfortable with and stick with that.

What I'm asking you to do to create your 100-page book is to dictate into a microphone for five hours. Don't you think that's better than typing for 48 hours?

Tip: While dictating a novel is possible, I find that I have to use a good, old fashioned keyboard to write fiction. Dictating might work to throw together a quick outline for a novel (I haven't done that), but not the whole enchilada.

It's okay to use different tools for different jobs.

For this job, for writing a nonfiction, memoir, or similar book, quickly, dictate it and it will work well.

Stop and Listen to Your Inner Self

Get those talking points settled in your mind. One thing is that, even though you'll have the talking point planned out, you're going to find that in due time you will change them, even with the most carefully laid plans. I'm a big advocate of creating a plan, creating an outline, having something in mind, but I'm an even bigger advocate of being open to new ideas, new thoughts, and new arrangements of those thoughts and ideas that will come to your mind—that will present themselves, often early in the morning or late at night.

And when those ideas come to you, don't ignore them. Pay attention. That is your inner self or your higher self, depending on how you want to term it, talking to you. And you want to pay attention to that. That's the part of yourself that's able to see a much bigger picture than your boxed-in conscious self and is able to take into account many details that you do not consciously recall or understand. So pay attention, trust yourself, and get those great ideas down so you can share them with others.

That's happened many times when I've been writing books, and it's happened for me when writing *this* book. I think that is because your book is for someone else, not you. You're writing it for someone out there in the wide world who needs *your* help.

I know a lot of people say that they write books only for themselves but isn't that kind of, well, selfish? Isn't this really something that you're doing to help somebody else? To share with them the information that you already have but which they don't have? Helping others is risky business. Don't preserve your ego in favor of the needs of others.

This is what this is really about and if you want this to get into a lot of people's hands, you've got to have the intent of sharing with others. And so because you're sharing with other people, there are forces that would like to get information into that book so that when a particular person finds that book they'll find answers that will be a blessing to their lives.

I know this may sound hippie-cosmic to some people but this is really the truth. This is how the universe, our world, works. There is great benevolence in this world that we live in. There are higher sources, there are higher powers than ourselves that are working to bring people together, to bring peace to the planet. In spite of all the discouraging things that you hear on the new, there can be peace on this planet and you can be part of that. You must be part of it.

Start Recording

Now it's time to start dictating your book. You no doubt at this point are going to discover some resistance rising up inside of you or from external sources.

When you make a decision to do something different—to make a change in your life or to undertake a big project—there is something that will happen inside your mind and body that will bring up resistance and fear.

This is a natural mechanism. It's there to protect you and to preserve your energy, but getting through it is the key.

Once you get on the other side of that resistance you'll find that it becomes easier and easier to find and take the time to do the dictation or "fast writing" that you need to do.

Like a Distance Runner

I'd like you to think about a runner for a moment. Perhaps you are a runner, you are a marathoner, or maybe you like to jog. If so, you'll understand this. There's a tremendous resistance in writing book just like there is for a distance runner.

But what happens is you force your body to do it. Other things are released in your body like chemicals and soon running becomes a pleasure and then an addiction. And I mean addiction in the kindest, most positive way in this context.

This is a lot like writing or any meaningful task that takes effort to get started. As you get started and put forth the right amount of effort, you get past that resistance and soon you'll be so excited about what you're doing that the resistance will fall off and will not rear it's puny, thin-skulled head anymore. Writer's block will not dog or hinder you.

That's why I emphasize putting in some real thought and effort as you begin recording your book.

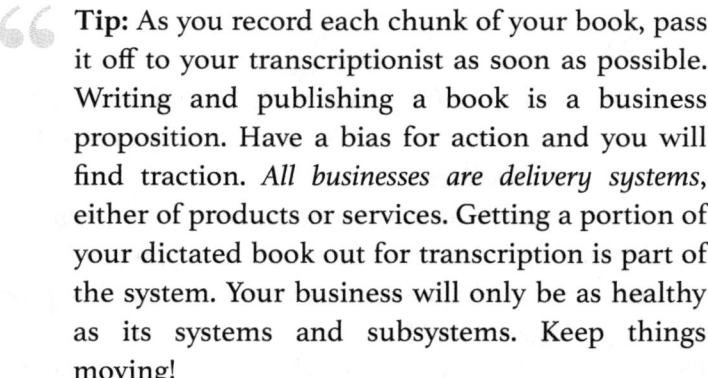**Tip:** As you record each chunk of your book, pass it off to your transcriptionist as soon as possible. Writing and publishing a book is a business proposition. Have a bias for action and you will find traction. *All businesses are delivery systems,* either of products or services. Getting a portion of your dictated book out for transcription is part of the system. Your business will only be as healthy as its systems and subsystems. Keep things moving!

STEP 5: ASSEMBLING AND FORMATTING YOUR BOOK

You have dictated your whole book and you've sent it out, piece by piece, for transcription. You've gotten the transcribed files back, hopefully in chunks as well, a few pages at a time.

> **Tip:** You wouldn't want to dictate the whole book into one single audio file. You certainly can do it but it would make it ungainly and you would have a hard time transporting that file around and managing it. So I advise recording it in short chunks. It will be easier on you.

You've got these chunks of your book and those chunks should be organized according to the outline of talking points that you developed earlier. Now start dropping them into a file.

My advice on this is very simple. Assemble your books in a Word template file. If you've got Microsoft Word, just put the text in a Word template file that you've put together or downloaded (see www.michaeljamesfitzgerald.com/resources.html).

You can do it in a lot of different ways, such as with Adobe

InDesign, but we're aiming at a shorter book, one that's about 20,000 to 40,000 words, and Word is sufficient. With that many words, it is likely that your book is going to be between 90 and 130 pages long.

 Tip: Microsoft Word has gotten better about handling large files. It used to be when I'd hit around 100 pages in a Word file that it would start acting up on me. It's not so bad in the most recent versions due, in part, I *think*, to the DOCX (XML) format. I have a really long file in Word format right now. A novel manuscript. It's 525 pages long at the moment and I haven't had any problems with it, not like I used to. I'm using a recent version of Word on the Mac. As for some of the older versions, I can't vouch for them. They may really go coo-coo on you. But since we're only going for a shorter book-length manuscript, we're going to be okay with recent versions of Word.

Other Formatting Options

If you are tech savvy and a bit adventurous, you might try, instead of Word, Amazon's free formatting tool, Kindle Create, which you can download it, for either the Mac or the PC, from https://www.amazon.com/Kindle-Create/b?node=18292298011. It will take some getting used to, but it really is a nice option.

Another option, and the one I use almost exclusivity now, is Vellum, available at Vellum.pub. It's for Mac only and costs a piece of change, but I've been using it for several years and I really like it.

But tackling a new piece of software is not what this is about. We are after speed. So, depending on your tech skills, dropping your newly minted book in a simple Word template may be the quickest, easiest way to go. Remember, you can grab several templates at www.michaeljamesfitzgerald.com/resources.html.

It is up to you, though. Please do what ever will go the quickest for you.

STEP 6: EDITING YOUR BOOK

Now that your book is dictated and assembled, it's time to start editing your book—to clean up your act, so to speak. You're going to self-edit and you're also going to get others to edit it, too.

Your grammar may not be the best, or your punctuation may not be perfect. I would not get uptight about that kind of thing.

Editing your book is a simple process and I'll tell you some things that have helped me over the years. I've been working as a writer and editor since the early 1980s and there's just a couple of practices that I do when self-editing that really help.

Two Basic Things

First of all, I read my text over several times and sometimes I might read it two or three times and be satisfied, sometimes I read it 20 times, depending on the book. You should read your dictated book several times, at least twice, but more times if you can squeeze it in.

Re-reading is part of your job as a writer. Don't shirk it.

I call this time spent with a manuscript "time in the Japanese garden." Time to let beauty have a word with you. It's best to listen when beauty speaks.

Another thing that really helps, and this is the second thing I do, is I read the text out loud to myself—either I read it out loud to myself or I have the computer read it back to me. (For example, on my Mac, I use the **Dictation and Speech** feature; see **System Preferences**.)

The reason why reading aloud helps me is that it lights up a different part of my brain, one that does not light up when I am reading silently.

When you're reading quietly, your brain is basically an energy-saving mechanism and so if it can guess that a word is there, it will just guess that it's there and skip over some words. Your brain can be lazy in that way. If it can conduct the right synapses to give you a meaning without actually seeing and registering the word, that's what's going to happen. So just reading the text quickly and silently is not always a great way to self-edit.

What I suggest is reading the book several times, at least twice, as I said, and either reading it to yourself out loud or having the computer read it back to you. And as this lights up different parts of your brain, you'll notice two (other) basic things. You'll notice that (1) if the words are not placed well it will sound funny and it will catch your attention in a different way than seeing it on the page will catch your attention, and (2) you'll sense the rhythm, the flow, and the meter of the book.

You don't want your book to sound jarring. It doesn't have to play like a beautiful piece of music to be valuable or useful, but it shouldn't be jarring or confusing to the reader. And that's another good reason to read it out loud because then you'll really be able to tell how your book sounds to the ear.

We're not trying to be Pablo Neruda here. I admire the work of Neruda tremendously. I wish I could write like that all the time—and I do believe with enough practice and enough heart you can.

The truth is that all of us can write extremely well. But for the book that we're creating here it's all about process and it's all about speed. We will maintain good quality but we are not so uptight about the quality of the manuscript that we can't move forward in a bold, swift way.

Remember done is better than perfect (Scott Allen)—and that's what we're after here—getting this done. Once you do this first book and you do it quickly, it's like you've run your first marathon. If you fared well and you did it right and followed best practices, it will be a thrilling experience for you. You'll be tired at the finish line but you'll want to do it over and over and over again.

I love what I do as a writer. That's what I've wanted to do since I was in my late teens. That was a long time ago, a very long time, and I still love it. This work of writing has been a guiding star through the desert of life.

I write every day—almost every day with very rare lapses. I will never retire from writing because I enjoy it so much—the great pleasure, the joy, and meaning that comes from self-expression. It's a gift and it's a gift that we should freely share with others. And that's why I'm sharing this book with you, to teach you some simple steps to begin expressing yourself and getting your message out. Quickly.

Your Editor

You've done your self-edit. It's now time to get one or more editors involved. Remember earlier in the book we talked about the selection of someone to help you read your book and check it for errors. You might know someone in the business that will give your book an honest look. And either you picked a professional who might be found through a place like

Upwork.com, Freelancer.com, or maybe even your local want ads.

Get in touch with them early in the process. Let them know you have work you are going to send their way. Have them take on little pieces of the book at a time. Serialize the work.

Don't wait until the whole book is put together before you hand over parts to edit and proofread. What you want to do is after you've organized the book into sections and larger sections (chapters) what I would do is take those chapters, as soon as they are ready, and give them to your editor.

Once again you may engage an editor who would only be checking punctuation, style, usage, basic grammar, and the like. This is called *copyediting*. A minimum or basic edit like this may prove adequate.

Often you need to make substantive changes, meaning that you will need them to take a deeper dive and make changes to structure, tone, style, and the like.

I also have dozens of friends, colleagues, and contacts who are great editors as well. If you would like help with one of my editor friends, please contact me at michaeljamesfitzgerald.com/contact.html.

There's a balance between delivery time and quality. What I don't want for any writer to do is to get caught up in the process of improving, improving, and improving the text. That could go on for an eternity if you are not careful. You will never stop making changes until you consciously stop it.

Ernest Hemingway once said, "There's nothing that's been written that couldn't be written better." So, even for him, there was a time to stop fiddling around and get the thing published.

You have to decide how far you're going to go in worrying about getting things just perfect. As I mentioned earlier, "Done is better than perfect" (Scott Allen).

For a book that you're trying to produce quickly, you want to have a baseline of quality, you want to make sure that you don't have misspelled any words or a string of words smushed into a single word or poor punctuation, those kinds of things, but be okay with imperfect.

So to not to annoy your reader, make sure the value of the material outweighs other considerations, such as perfect punctuation. What will it matter if the book is perfectly edited but the material is not valuable to readers? This is of critical importance if you actually want to sell books: create value, not perfection. Value is tangible; perfection, intangible.

There are lots of beautifully edited and designed books out there that few will read because the material between their covers is not valuable.

You'll be surprised how much people will forgive in exchange for real, redeemable value.

Work together with your editors. Accept criticism readily from them. Consider them reliable sources, and if you have picked your editors well, they will be a blessing. Send them your book in parts. Most will accept you book in parts. It will keep things moving along.

Incorporate those edits with energy, vigor, and determination, then move on to the next steps.

STEP 7: PUBLISH AND PROMOTE YOUR BOOK

Hear that? Your book is revving its engine. You've got it formatted using Kindle Create or a simple Word template, like I shared with you in Step 5 a few chapters ago. You have found a designer for your cover, such as on Fiverr.com, or you've designed a decent cover yourself on Canva.com. You've read and reread it, and it has been reviewed by an editor or two several times. It's been proofread, and it's been 24 hours well spent. You're ready to publish your book!

Now that you've got all these parts together, this is what I would do. Here is the first horse out of the chute: Go back to Amazon's Kindle Direct Publishing at kdp.amazon.com, log in with your Amazon credentials, and start creating your book. It's a very easy place to publish and sell your and earn a 35 to 70 percent royalty. Upload your cover, upload your text, preview (under "Preview Your Book" on the KDP site) and make sure that it flows well and looks good. In a matter of hours it will appear on an Amazon page. You will be a published author.

Later, you'll want to create a paperback edition of your book. You can do that on KDP, but make that secondary for your 24-hour goal. You could also use sites like Lulu.com or IngramSpark.com print paperback or hardcover books. But

Later, yet again, choose to publish your book on other platforms as well, such as:

- iTunes Connect (see www.apple.com/itunes/working-itunes/sell-content/connect)
- Press.BarnesandNoble.com
- Kobo.com
- Smashwords.com

 Tip: If you enroll your book in KDP Select (see https://kdp.amazon.com/en_US/select), you have have to commit to exclusivity on Amazon for a certain period of time. It is usually worth it for because of the extra royalties you get from page reads through Kindle Unlimited (see https://www.amazon.com/kindle-dbs/hz/subscribe/ku). But stay open to other opportunities, that is, other platforms.

Selling Your Book

I want to talk to you now about how to sell your book. If you've published your book on Amazon.com it's visible to the whole world. (By the way, you won't be limited to selling you book just on Amazon.com; you can set up your book to sell in other markets as well, such as Australia, the UK, and many other countries. Why not? You'll see instructions on this for on you book's "pricing" page on KDP.)

But how will people know where to find your book if you don't tell them where?

That's why you'll want to promote your book through social

media. That's why I suggested early on that you get accounts on Twitter, Facebook, and so forth.

But I caution you, once again, not to get carried away with B UY MY BOOK! BUY MY BOOK! syndrome. People get turned off and will drop you. But do share your excitement and be generous, like telling people when your book is discounted or free for a certain period of time. Share excerpts. Offer to help people. When they trust you and your product, they will be more than happy to buy. It takes time.

What you want to share on these social media sites is a link to where people can find your book. Your link to your book on Amazon will be long, so it's often useful to use a shortened link, especially when you are limited to 140 characters on Twitter.

> **Tip:** I have created shortened links, such as on Bit.ly, to track clicks. It lets me track how many clicks that link has gotten and other interesting bits of information.

It's also nice to have your own website to promote your books. I don't know how to design a website very well—that's not my forte. And it can be rather expensive to hire a contractor to create a site for you. WordPress.com is a simple, easy to use solution for that, but we're not going to go off on that here.

Marketing Your Book

I'd suggest at this point that take your marketing efforts seriously. There's a couple of things that you can do inexpensively, for free actually, that will be important to uploading your book online.

As described earlier, you can create a Facebook business page, set up a Twitter account, get on Pinterest, SlideShare,

LinkedIn, and YouTube. Create a blog on either Blogger or WordPress (preferred). Share part of what makes you *you* with the world. Follow others and support them and help them share their ideas. Be a good digital citizen, a positive force for good.

Find hashtags that match your message and use them. If you know nothing or little about hashtags, go to Udemy.com and find a course on hashtags and other marketing techniques, such as blogging and advertising on Amazon or Facebook.

You have to get yourself out there. You have to broaden your circle. You have to be unafraid to say, "Hey, I've got something for you. Check it out!"

Don't be afraid to make new friends or to do favors for others. Make friends with other writers and promote their books. Ask your friends to post links to your blog posts on their social media.

Thing big. Think huge. Go global. Go ballistic.

(Psst! But please don't wear out your welcome by being overly salesy.)

> **Tip:** You might already have signed up on these sites and if you have, that's good. You should, however, consider whether you want to use your personal accounts for business. You should think about whether or not you want to have separate accounts —professional accounts—for promoting books or if you want to just keep everything on your personal accounts. It's up to you. I like keeping things separate.

Using Blogger for Your Website

So back to the website business. What I do is I let the ideas for domain names come to me and I also register the domain with my Internet provider and then, if I feel it is a go, one thing I have done is use Blogger to set up a blog there for that domain name. I redirect that $8–$12 a year website or domain name that I've registered and have that redirect that to my Blogger blog.

Set up a blog on Blogger.com and then redirect your domain to that blog. This link shows you how: https://support.google.com/blogger/answer/1233387.

 Tip: I know there's a lot of back and forth out there about whether WordPress is better than Blogger and that it gets better traffic than Blogger. Yes, it certainly is better in several ways, but I'm sharing my preference for Blogger with you because it's really easy to use even though I know it doesn't have some of the advantages of WordPress.

WordPress definitely has some tremendous advantages, especially for someone who is knowledgeable about web design. If you want to use WordPress because you're already comfortable there and that's where you've had experience, I say go for it. It costs a little money.

If you have a hole in your purse, go with Blogger. It's very simple to use. You can easily choose a different design, a different background picture, create your own logo for the top of the page, do all kinds of things to make your blogging life easy. I use WordPress now, but I have used both, but I prefer Blogger.

Blog Posts

Here is a simple way that you can promote your book on your blog: Take excerpts from your book and use them for blog posts. Then use social media to share links back to your blog.

> **Tip:** Ask friends and family members to post your link on their social media. Create a short post about your book, then offer a promotion, such as a free book for a limited time, or a reduced price "today only." If you word your tweets and status updates right—not pushy but open, kind, smart, or helpful—they won't find them offensive to share, and you'll broaden your marketing reach by thousands.

Using social media is very easy to do. However, if you don't know how to do it, I can guarantee you that somewhere in your network of family and friends, especially younger friends—teenagers and people in their 20s—know how to do this kind of thing. It's natural to the millennials and post-millennials.

Use your blog not only as a venue for promotion but a place to sell your book. Get an associates account on Amazon (affiliate-program.amazon.com) and then post banners and links to your book (and perhaps others). You will find instructions on how to do this on Amazon's affiliate program web site linked above.

And all of this is free except for the cost of the domain name which is less than $15.00.

Running Ads on Amazon and Facebook

This is a huge topic, out of scope for this thin, starter volume. But it will be worth it to learn more. My suggestion is to go to

YouTube.com and search for videos on Amazon and Facebook ads for beginners.

But the least I can do . . . is leave you with a quick, minimal, cheap bit of advice on how to get started with a low-budget Amazon ad:

1. Create a list of 100 to 500 keywords related to your book—go to Google Keyword Planner (https://ads.google.com/home/tools/keyword-planner/) to find them
2. Get set up on advertising.Amazon.com
3. Click **Create Campaign**
4. Choose **Sponsored Products**
5. Name your campaign something you won't regret
6. Set the start and end dates for you campaign
7. Set a daily budget (try $3.00 to $5.00 or even a single buck to start)
8. Pick **Manual Targeting** so you can use your own keywords
9. Use **Dynamic bids—down only** to start
10. You'll be presented with your book to select for your ad (or a list of books, depending on how many you have published, both e-books and paperback)
11. Under **Creative,** write a short, snappy, mesmerizingly inviting ad for your book in 150 characters or less
12. Under **Keyword Targeting**, upload your keywords in the Excel template Amazon provides (you have to download it first, of course—you'll find it under **Upload File**)
13. To start, just use "Broad" as your match type for now —you can add more match types later
14. Bid each keyword at $0.10 or less (I usually use $0.07

or $0.08 to start and raise the bids on well performing keywords after a week or so)
15. Don't worry about negative keywords yet
16. Set your default bid to $0.10 or less (yes, cheap)
17. Launch your campaign
18. Come to your Amazon ad page regularly to monitor (especially if you set no end date for you ad)

No, I didn't explain much about what you were doing there with Amazon ads, but you got your feet wet. Now the learning about Amazon ads begins!

PITFALL PIT-STOP

I'm going to take a few pages to cover some pitfalls that will magically appear while you are in the process of creating a book.

Perfectionism

Being a perfectionist gets in the way of you making progress in life. Voltaire said, "The perfect is the enemy of the good." In other words, perfectionism is a distraction from the real goal.

If you are a perfectionist, that likely means you're looking at writing as a means for acceptance by others. And if you're using writing for acceptance, in my opinion, you may be in pursuit of a selfish version of love, a very dissatisfying, empty sort of love, which, I am afraid, is not love at all.

What you want to do is you want to give a gift to others and you want to be unafraid to give that gift even though it's imperfect. See, that's the way love works. Love is an imperfect gift that we give to each other and writing a book is an example of that.

Don't be afraid. If your heart is in it, if you're really trying to help somebody else with the information you're providing, then you're not going to go wrong, even if the book isn't just right. And even if not everyone likes it.

Your version of "just right" will change daily. You can't catch up with it. You have to decide when you're done. Don't let an arbitrary concept of what perfection is hold you back.

I remember hearing a story about a man and I don't remember who it was but he created a series of videos and a book to go along with it. And he went to great effort to make it as beautiful and as professional as he possibly could. The result was gorgeous, but he didn't sell very many of copies of his program.

And then someone encouraged him to take a sort of underground guerrilla approach. "I'm going to change the look and feel of this book and my videos. I'm going to make it look like it's a notebook that I've reproduced in my basement, and it's going to have stains on the cover, but the content is going to be awesome."

Or words to that effect. The result was that he sold millions of dollars' worth of his book and the accompanying videos. He understood that readers (and viewers) are looking for something of value and they will overlook faults because of their gratitude for the valuable, much needed information.

Perfection can put people off. You want to invite them in and relate to them so you can help them and serve them.

Don't worry so much that it reads and looks perfect. It doesn't have to. What it does need is the unique brushwork of your heart and soul. You need to break off a piece of your heart and soul and offer it as a gift to others. When you do that, it will make a difference in their lives. It will touch them and it will move them and they'll be better for it and so will you.

Work Quickly

When you get changes back from your editor, incorporate those changes quickly. One thing I've learned about being edited over the years is that I really don't resist many suggestions that come my way anymore. I figure that the people that I've asked to read my material are either great professionals or good enough friends that they're just going to tell me the truth.

I'm going to pay them to tell me the truth and I'm going to love them for telling me the truth. The truth is a wonderful thing. Listen to it. One of the signs of an immature artist or writer is the desire to preserve ego over a chance at making things better.

Don't make that mistake.

I'm not talking about an extreme where someone comes along and completely reinvents everything that you write. Don't tolerate that. But when a trustworthy editor comes your way with good ideas and says, "You know, it's going to be clearer if you word it this way." Accept it. Enter the changes in your file and move on. Quickly. That's my suggestion to you.

Keep Believing in Yourself

About this time, you are in the throes of working with the text that you've created through dictation and transcription. You're in the phase of reorganizing your book and having it edited or proofread and this is a time when doubts infect the mind. Quite understandable.

Whenever you're trying to move forward in your life—this is when you find that opposition arises to distract you from what you're trying to accomplish— especially if what you're trying to accomplish is going to be bringing good into the lives of others.

If that's your intent, deep in your heart, you will overcome all opposition; if you have mixed intent—for example, if you are doing this only in the pursuit of money or for selfish reasons—you'll feel mixed up about it and you won't produce your best work. If money is a by-product of your cause, your cause being a love of others and a desire to share part of yourself with them, then you will find it much easier to believe in yourself and believe in what you're trying to accomplish.

If your intent is distorted by a mix of doubt and fear and a need for adulation, you'll find that your way will be hedged up. You won't prosper in your business like you would hope.

Now I'm not saying that it's wrong to desire money because it isn't. We have to have money and the more of it the better, if you can handle it. The key here is how you handle it.

How do you handle money? Here's what I think: Appreciate it, use it to do good, but don't get attached to it. Be willing to let it go at any moment for something more valuable.

Just because you're writing a book doesn't mean you're going to become famous. You could enjoy a small bit of fame or if you are particularly insightful and delightful in your writing and you give people a lot of joy and satisfaction, you could become famous. But what is your goal? What is your main desire?

If your main desire, and this is my point, is to help other people, to bless and uplift their lives, to help them get what they want in life, then it's going to be natural to believe in yourself. If you believe in yourself, you're going to be able to carry out your plans to the fullest and be successful in accomplishing exactly what you set out to do.

A FINAL WORD

Our time together is nearly over. I've almost finished dictating (writing) this book.

I want to congratulate you for what you've accomplished in reading this book. You now know exactly how to write, publish, and promote your book in 24 hours. If you follow in detail the steps that I've given you, it can even take you even less time.

I've produced this book and several others in less than 24 hours. And one of the reasons I know that is because I've kept close track of everything I've done. Not just writing, editing, dictating, and cover creation, but everything I've done—from uploading files to sending emails—I kept track of everything. And the total number came to 23 and a half hours, a little under my stated goal.

> **Note:** I recorded most of the work I did on this book in exact minutes; however, I had to do some estimation (I always overestimated in that case) because the notebook where I kept track of my work was stolen from a rental car in in Chinatown San Francisco. Life lesson.

I did not do this in a full physical day. No, I didn't sit down on a Friday at 5:00 a.m. and do all of this work and then publish my book at 5:00 a.m. on Saturday. I spread the work out.

I spread it out because I had to. I've got other responsibilities just like you've got responsibilities. I've got a job that I really enjoy and a family to care for and plenty of things to do for other people.

But, nevertheless, I have a goal to write and publish a book in 24 contiguous hours (or less) in the future. I believe it's possible, and it sounds like my kind of fun. But I'll need to ramp up.

I wish you all the best in the sales of your book and I hope you influence other people for good as you share your message with them.

I hope your interest in sharing part of yourself goes beyond self-interest—not giving away your book for free but willing to make an exchange for the value of what you've created to benefit others.

I hope that you believe in yourself a little more than when you started reading this book. I hope that you are persistent—consistently persistent—and that you don't give up. That you keep working, keep trying, keep listening to that pure voice inside of you that gives you ideas about things that you can do to improve your life and the lives of others.

I believe in action, and I believe in taking inspired action, though I haven't always taken decisive action.

Yes, good things come to those who wait but good things also come more predictably to those who take action.

And I'm not talking about just work, because we can work and work and work and *work* and not get what we're aiming to get. But I'm talking about taking the right actions at the right time and following the inner voice that comes to every single one of us.

Your Inner Voice

We have a need to trust that voice and understand what that voice is. And if you don't know what that voice is, a lot of people will call it a lot of different things. Some people will call it "my higher self" or "my higher purpose." Some people call it "source" and all kinds of other things. I personally believe it's a voice from a heavenly Being speaking to my spirit.

You have to train yourself to listen to what that voice is saying and to not listen to what appeals to your vanity and pride or an inclination to underestimate your abilities. You have to learn through trial and error and practice whether the voice you are hearing is a true voice and what that true voice saying to you. Then you have to develop the courage to follow through by taking the action on those promptings.

Your Thoughts

If you want to be able to pluck fruit off a tree from your own orchard, you've got to plant the tree. You've got to water the tree. You've got to care for the tree while it's young and tender. You've got to fertilize it. You've got to prune it. You've got to take good care of it.

I compare the tree to the network of thoughts and ideas that come to me and you.

Each one of those thoughts or ideas is a branch and if all those lines of thinking are branches then maybe each idea is a leaf. There can be so many ideas that you cannot count them but don't let them dry up on the branch. You want to take good care of the tree and make sure that that tree can bear fruit and then you can pluck and eat the harvest it bears.

And so to do that you've got to take right action. You can't do that if you are hanging onto your blurry past. You've got to be able to forgive yourself for making wrong choices while you're learning. You need to set them aside. Don't look at your wrong actions or negative thoughts as something to pull you down or discourage you or to make you angry. Don't let them do that to you. Be grateful for your learning experiences. Be grateful that the experience of failure has come to you to teach you one of the wrong ways to go or one of the wrong ways to do things. If you look at your life this way, you will always see past any failure.

Because you are publishing your book Amazon Kindle and perhaps, later, on other platforms, you still have complete editorial control over your book. You can simply edit your book file if you've found an error that you need to correct. You fix it, upload the new draft, then your corrected draft is available almost immediately. Even though you've gone forward boldly, your chance to change your book is not behind you. You can correct the problems that you may have overlooked when you first published the book.

Your Post-Mortem

After you've been through the process once, hold a little post-mortem meeting with yourself, with your collaborators, or whoever you want, and see what worked for you and what didn't. Then improve upon it and create your own process to create a book based on your personal experience.

If you do this, if you document what went wrong and how you can improve it, then nine times out of 10, the next time you do it your time will be much shorter, your time to market much improved.

And if you prove yourself as a willing messenger, one who is prepared to share you message with great energy, who is willing to take ideas, inspired ideas and take them from the dust of the earth and create something out of them, you are going to be a very happy person and a very successful person.

Keep going. Don't let discouragement rule your life. Keep fighting for what you really believe in, for your amazing ideas and lofty ideals, for what you believe is your true purpose in life. You'll be happy that you did.

I wish you the greatest success.

APPENDIX

WRITE YOUR BOOK IN 24 HOURS CHECKLIST

These estimates total from a range of about 10.5 hours to 22 hours. Some tasks will take longer than expected, others much shorter, depending on experience, distraction, and other factors. The times in the subheadings are rounded up or down.

Introduction (10-20 Minutes)

1. Analyze why you want to write a book (10–20 minutes)

Preparation (3.5-5 Hours)

1. Identify and hire a transcriptionist (one or more) on Upwork.com for example or sign up for a transcription service such as Rev.com or download its app (20–30 minutes)
2. Identify and recruit or hire one or more copy editors and/or proofreaders (15–30 minutes)

3. Set up a Google Drive account or similar (10 minutes)
4. Set up account on Kindle Direct Publishing (20 minutes)
5. Decide what your book is about and who its target audience is (10–20 minutes)
6. Decide on a working title (5–10 minutes)
7. Begin creating a book cover on Canva.com or put the cover out for bid on 99designs.com or similar site (30–60 minutes)
8. Create a list of initial talking points in random order (20 min)
9. Revise the order of your talking points into a loose outline (15 minutes)
10. Create a recording plan (5—10 minutes)
11. Create or download a book template or download Kindle Create (5–20 minutes)
12. Optional: Create slides from your talking points (20 minutes)
13. Optional: Purchase a digital audio recorder or better, just start practicing with your smartphone's default voice recorder (10 minutes)
14. Optional: Create a social media accounts for future marketing communication (10 minutes)
15. Optional: Create a blog on Blogger WordPress if you don't already have one (10–15 minutes)

Writing (2.5 to 7 hours)

1. Dictate book content based on your talking points (2–6 hours, in 15–30 minute increments)
2. Upload recorded audio files for transcriptionist or to your transcription service (10–30 minutes)

3. Begin assembling your book in the template as dictation files start coming back to you (5–20 minutes)

Editing (2–3 Hours)

1. Edit and reorganize your book, and add headings (30 minutes)
2. Send parts of your book to your copy editor and/or proofreader for editing and review (5–15 minutes)
3. Incorporate changes from your editor or proofreader (30–60 minutes)
4. Review final, edited copy of your book (30–60 minutes)
5. Finalize your book cover (20 minutes)

Publishing (2–2.5 Hours)

1. Finish your e-book cover (30–60 minutes)
2. Publish your book on Amazon Kindle using the front cover (30 minutes)
3. Later: Publish your book on as a paperback after creating a full-sized cover—the front cover is the same for both the e-book and the paperback (20-30 minutes)
4. Later: Publish your book in hardcover, if you like, on Lulu.com or IngramSpark.com or a similar site (20–30 minutes)

Marketing (1 to 4 Hours)

1. Promote your book on social media sites (5–60 minutes)
2. Write one or more blog posts about your book (2–60 minutes)
3. Promote your blog posts on social media and ask friends and family to share your posts on their social media (5–60 minutes)
4. Optional: Create ads on Amazon or Facebook (30–60)

ABOUT THE AUTHOR

Michael James Fitzgerald likes to write, read, and run. He doesn't own a television—he prefers doing something creative. He is the author of over 20 books that have been published worldwide, with translations in Spanish, Portuguese, French, German, Polish, Korean, Japanese, and Chinese. You can find more about him at MichaelJamesFitzgerald.com.

ALSO BY MICHAEL JAMES FITZGERALD

As a Man Thinketh Workbook Edition
by James Allen with Michael James Fitzgerald
The Science of Getting Rich Workbook Edition
by Wallace D. Wattles with Michael James Fitzgerald
Making Decisions: With the Reflection Method
by Michael James Fitzgerald

www.ingramcontent.com/pod-product-compliance
Lightning Source LLC
Chambersburg PA
CBHW071305040426
42444CB00009B/1876